TATE MODERN
HIGHLIGHTS

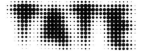

FOREWORD

Welcome to Tate Modern. We are a museum of international art from 1900 to the present day. Since opening in 2000 – the youngest in the family of Tate galleries – we have dedicated our collection displays and exhibition programmes to continuously refresh our understanding of the past, from the perspective of the present.

Over the last twenty years Tate's international collection has grown and evolved from its original core in modern European and American art into a collection that responds to an intricate network of artistic practice across the world. Works on display in our galleries now represent the endeavours of artists from over forty countries. Exhibitions and commissions in the Turbine Hall and the Tanks enable new works to be shown for the first time, allowing artists to challenge both themselves and their audiences, who will encounter some of the most interesting and dynamic art in the world.

Traditionally museums have set out their collections according to a chronological history. From the outset, Tate Modern has adopted a different approach, now widely emulated, in which works of art are displayed in thematic groupings and thought-provoking pairings. Experiencing art within such fresh contexts helps to expand our understanding of past and present from many different perspectives. In the Natalie Bell Building you will find four collection displays arranged in rooms that bring out rich histories and interconnections between artworks, as well as focusing on solo artists. The Blavatnik Building, which opened in 2016, has a more contemporary focus. The displays here explore performance and participatory practices in art since the 1960s and the Tanks are dedicated to live art and time-based media. On level 5, Tate Exchange provides a space that is open for everyone to experiment and participate in a programme that discovers new perspectives on life, through art.

Visitors bring to their understanding of art a combination of their own knowledge and lived experience, and Tate Modern aims to provide a positive and supportive environment for all. The texts in the displays and in this publication are intended to provide useful information rather than to tell visitors what to think: we hope everybody will enjoy deepening their understanding by asking questions and finding their own connections and associations. For first-time visitors the *Start Display* offers an introduction to the museum and a taste of how you will see the works displayed in the rest of the building. For those who are already familiar with Tate Modern we hope every visit to our ever-changing displays will encourage you to look again and think again.

This book is intended as a helpful guide to the museum, or a memento of your visit. It documents some important moments from our twenty-year history and highlights a small selection of the remarkable works of art in our displays. These works have been chosen to include not only a number of much-loved favourites, but also as a range of either less well-known or more recently acquired works that we believe will provide visitors with a fascinating and memorable visit and an insight into our vision.

Frances Morris
Director, Tate Modern

Phyllida Barlow, *untitled: upturnedhouse2* 2012

TURBINE HALL

Originally housing the electricity generators in Bankside Power Station, the Turbine Hall is a vast public space.

Since 2000, it has become one of the gallery's most distinctive features, providing the setting for some of the most spectacular and talked-about artworks of the twenty-first century. Initially sponsored by Unilever, a range of international artists have created a series of specially commissioned works for the Turbine Hall. Louise Bourgeois constructed the towers *I Do, I Undo, I Redo*, and placed the twelve-metre-high spider *Maman* on the bridge. Anish Kapoor filled the whole length of the space with *Marsyas*. With Olafur Eliasson's *The Weather Project*, the sun seemed to peer down through a hazy mist. *Test Site* by Carsten Höller installed five giant slides. Doris Salcedo broke open a crevice in the floor of the museum with *Shibboleth*, and Ai Weiwei installed a sea of porcelain *Sunflower Seeds*. A new series of Turbine Hall commissions, sponsored by Hyundai Motor, began in 2015 with Abraham Cruzvillegas's *Empty Lot*, followed in 2016 by Philippe Parreno and *Anywhen*. The Danish collective SUPERFLEX installed a series of multi-user swings across the Turbine Hall in 2017, and in 2018 Tania Bruguera focused attention on migration, our emotional response and the power of collective action. With a new bridge on level 4, linking the main buildings, the Turbine Hall remains at the heart of Tate Modern.

This page: Olafur Eliasson, *The Weather Project* 2003 (top); Doris Salcedo, *Shibboleth* 2007 (bottom). Opposite page: Anish Kapoor, *Marsyas* 2002 (top left); Tania Bruguera, *Tatlin's Whisper #5* 2008 (top right); Rachel Whiteread, *EMBANKMENT* 2005 (centre left); Tacita Dean *Film* 2011 (centre right); Ai Weiwei, *Sunflower Seeds* 2010 (bottom right); Dominique Gonzalez-Foerster, *TH.2058* 2008 (bottom centre); Carsten Höller, *Test Site* 2006 (bottom left).

Seeds

NATALIE BELL BUILDING

The Natalie Bell Building was named after a local community leader as part of a Turbine Hall commission by artist Tania Bruguera. It includes one floor for ticketed exhibitions and two floors of free displays of work from the Tate collection, entitled *Four Approaches to Modern Art (1900 to Now)*.

Each of the free displays looks at a distinct aspect of modern and contemporary art, bringing together a wide variety of works from different periods and different parts of the world.

Level 2 includes the *Start Display*, an introductory space that has been designed particularly for the first-time visitor. *In the Studio* focuses on the often intensely personal experience of making and looking at art, and *Artist and Society* shows artworks that address broader social and political issues.

On level 4, *Media Networks* examines the ways in which artists have responded to developments in media and communications technology, while *Materials and Objects* highlights the extraordinary range of materials and techniques used by artists over the last 120 years.

START DISPLAY

The *Start Display* is an introductory space, intended for people visiting a museum of modern art for the first time.

Presenting a selection of major works from the Tate collection, it encourages different ways of looking at art, and suggests helpful questions that you can ask yourself as you are walking around the rest of the museum.

The works in the *Start Display* are linked by a focus on colour, and these rooms highlight artworks from a range of countries, cultures and times. Including examples of painting, sculpture, collage and conceptual art, the display explores how we perceive colour, the connections between colour and memory, and the emotional or spiritual values that we assign to different colours.

Henri Matisse
The Snail 1953

Matisse began to make cut-outs when he was too ill to make paintings. Often confined to his bed or a wheelchair, he would cut shapes from sheets of paper painted in bright colours, which were positioned on the wall according to his instructions. 'The contour of the figure springs from the discovery of the scissors that give it the movement of circulating life', he explained. Here the rotating paper shapes radiate out in a spiral, echoing a snail's shell, to form what Matisse described as 'abstraction rooted in reality'.

Ceal Floyer
Monochrome Till Receipt (White) 1999

Floyer regularly challenges our preconceptions of what a work of art should be. Displayed on the wall of the gallery is a till receipt from a local supermarket. The items listed on the receipt are all linked by a single colour: they are all white or have the word 'white' in their name. The receipt itself is of little value and would ordinarily be thrown away. Here, however, it represents a conceptual still life in which the objects themselves exist, but are nowhere to be seen.

Gerhard Richter
Strip (921–6) 2011

Richter likes to explore new ways of
making paintings. *Strip (921–6)* is based
on an abstract painting from 1990. This
earlier work was made by passing a
squeegee over thick layers of paint,
pulling colours up and down, erasing
some and allowing others to resurface.
Twenty years later he photographed the
painting to create a digital image. Using
a computer programme he divided the
colours and stretched them out into a
series of horizontal strips. Produced as
a digital print and laminated onto
aluminium, it carries no trace of the
artist's hand.

IN THE STUDIO

In the Studio is about the close engagement of the individual with an artwork – whether making it or looking at it.

The image of an artist in his or her studio suggests that they have shut themselves off from the world to allow a period of intensive concentration. Of course, artists work in different ways, and in many different environments. An artwork can be made in a foundry, in a darkroom, or in the middle of a field. Nor does it have to be a solitary act. Some works based on performance or social interaction could involve hundreds of participants. Yet there are artists whose work is profoundly inward-looking, who depict the details of their domestic lives, or even – like some of the surrealists – explore their own subconscious as a source of images.

Just as making a work of art requires concentrated engagement, so too can the act of looking at one. Mark Rothko's Seagram murals were famously donated to Tate because the artist felt that the restaurant for which they were originally intended would not be a suitable setting for them. He wanted his paintings to be seen in an enclosed space that would encourage a more immersive and contemplative experience.

Art can also make us aware of the complexity of seeing, emphasising the psychological or philosophical influences on our perception, whether using optical effects that dazzle and disrupt our vision, or introducing distorted forms that seem to convey a profound sense of unease.

Georges Braque
Mandora 1909–10

Braque painted several still lifes featuring musical instruments during the winter of 1909–10. This was part of the critical period when he and Pablo Picasso worked closely together, establishing a technique of painting known as cubism that could suggest a series of shifting perspectives. A mandora is a small instrument similar to a lute, and the fragmented surface of the painting has its own musical quality, creating a shimmering sense of movement and rhythm.

Dod Procter
Morning 1926

This sleeping girl has a monumental
presence. Her supine figure fills the
unusually shaped canvas. Under the pale
early light her skin is like marble, while
the white folds of her clothing against the
white sheets resemble the finely worked
drapery of a classical sculpture. Originally
from London, Procter was one of many
artists who settled in Cornwall, attracted
by the distinctive quality of light. *Morning*
was exhibited at the Royal Academy
Summer Exhibition in 1927 and voted
by the public as the 'picture of the year';
it was bought for the nation by the *Daily
Mail* newspaper.

Salvador Dalí
Metamorphosis of Narcissus 1937

Dalí was fascinated by double images and
curious resemblances between apparently
different objects. In this painting the
doubling represents a magical moment
of transformation. The kneeling figure on
the left is Narcissus, a character in Greek
mythology who fell in love with his own
reflection and pined away. After his death,
the gods immortalised him as a flower,
which sprouts out of the egg clutched
between the raised fingers on the right.

Leonor Fini
Little Hermit Sphinx 1948

Fini's image of the Sphinx (a mythological hybrid of a lion and a woman) can be seen partly as a self-portrait. She regarded the Sphinx as a symbolic intermediary between the human and animal realms, and between the conscious mind and the deeper recesses of the imagination. Her position, crouched in the doorway of a decrepit building, similarly suggests a threshold between different states of being. A human lung is suspended from a lintel, while the figure toys with the scattered bones of a bird.

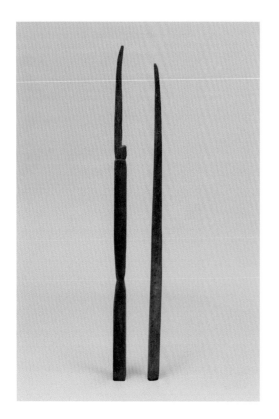

Louise Bourgeois
KNIFE COUPLE 1949

This work belongs to a series of carved wooden sculptures that Bourgeois made in the 1940s and 1950s. When she exhibited them they were arranged in clusters, as if they were interacting with each other. Bourgeois was intrigued by sharp objects such as knives or scissors, which could be threatening but were also instruments of creativity. *KNIFE COUPLE* can be seen as a psychologically charged and highly ambivalent image of a romantic relationship – two figures bound together by their willingness to cut and stab the outside world, or each other.

Shafic Abboud
Composition c.1957–8

In the 1950s, Abboud often worked by laying paint thickly onto the canvas, applying and shaping it with a palette knife to create an intense sense of movement. He was born in Lebanon, but spent most of his life in Paris, where this work was made. The blues and greys in this abstract painting seem to carry memories of the light and colour of his homeland.

Mark Rothko
Black on Maroon 1958

In the late 1950s, Rothko was commissioned
to paint a series of murals for the
fashionable Four Seasons restaurant,
in the Seagram Building on Park Avenue,
New York City. As he worked, however, the
murals assumed a more sober character,
dominated by maroon, dark red and black.
Recognising that a high-end restaurant
was not the ideal location for such a work,
Rothko withdrew from the commission
and finally presented the series to the Tate
Gallery. Displayed as the artist intended,
in reduced light and in a compact space,
the subtlety of the layered surfaces slowly
emerges, revealing their solemn and
meditative character.

Judit Reigl
Guano 1958–62

Early in her career Reigl was interested
in automatism – an approach to art
associated with surrealism, in which the
making of marks on the canvas or the
page is guided by the unconscious. This
painting belonged to a group of rejected
canvases that covered the floor of her
studio. Over time, drips and splashes of
paint fell onto their surfaces, building up
into thick encrustations. Eventually Reigl
returned to these canvases, scraping
back the layers of paint, and allowing
the resulting raking lines to remain visible.
The title relates to the excrement of
seabirds, which accumulates on rocks
and is gathered for fertiliser.

[handwritten annotations: "of" / "trees" / "roots ↑" / "egypt"]

Lee Krasner
Gothic Landscape 1961

Although this is an abstract painting,
the thick vertical lines that dominate its
centre can be seen as trees, with thick
knotted roots at their base. It was probably
this that led Krasner to call the painting
Gothic Landscape, several years after
completing it. *Gothic Landscape* was made
in the years following the death of her
husband Jackson Pollock in a car crash in
1956. It belongs to a series of large
canvases whose violent and expressive
gestural brushstrokes reflected her
feelings of grief.

Ibrahim El-Salahi
*Reborn Sounds of
Childhood Dreams I* 1961–5

El-Salahi studied painting in Khartoum
in the late 1940s, before completing his
studies in London. Returning to Khartoum
in 1957, he realised that Sudan – a newly
independent country in the midst of a civil
war – required a different approach in
his art. As one of the founders of the
Khartoum School, he developed a new
visual vocabulary comprising simple
forms, strong lines and sombre colours
inspired by his environment and rooted
in Arabic and African art and writing.

Germaine Richier

Chessboard, Large Version
(Original Painted Plaster) 1959

These five grotesque figures represent the
principal pieces in a game of chess: the
King, Queen, Knight, Castle and Bishop. The
Knight has a horse's head, while the Bishop
(known in France as the Fool) resembles
a hunchbacked jester. The pieces were
originally made as small figures in clay, then
modelled on a larger scale in plaster and
painted by the artist. Richier's distorted
animal and partly human figures reflect
the anxieties and despair of Europe after
the Second World War. 'Our age, when
you consider it, is full of talons', she said.
'It seems to me that in violent works there
is just as much sensibility as in poetic
ones. There can be just as much wisdom
in violence as in gentleness.'

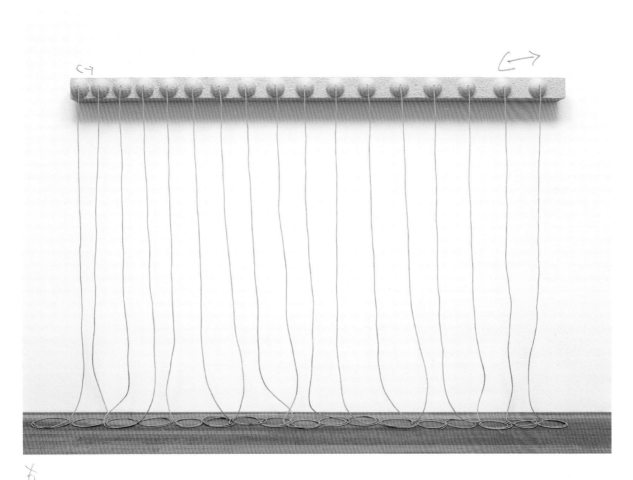

Eva Hesse
Addendum 1967

Hesse's approach to sculpture thrived
on contradictions. She would put hard and
soft materials together, geometric
shapes alongside more organic elements.
She was working at a time when many
American sculptors organised their work
according to prearranged systems as
a way of avoiding personal expression.
In *Addendum*, the circular papier-mâché
forms are positioned in a row according
to a mathematical sequence, so that the
distance between each one becomes
incrementally larger. The cords beneath
them are of identical length. However,
the sculpture is always installed at a set
height so that the cords curl unpredictably
on the ground beneath it.

ARTIST
AND
SOCIETY

This display looks at some of the ways in which artists engage with the world around them.

In the first half of the twentieth century, some artists believed that there was an implicit parallel between the development of a new visual language in modern art and the promise of a new society. The clean lines and balanced compositions of abstract painting and sculpture seemed to correspond to the utopian ideals of the time. Then, as the world descended into brutality and war, artists felt impelled to bear witness to the horrors and to remember the victims.

Art can also provide a powerful means of protesting against social injustice or drawing attention to those who have campaigned to change the world. Sometimes directly and sometimes more obliquely, artists have commemorated the heroes of the battle against apartheid in South Africa, the civil rights struggle in the United States, and the women's rights movement in India. Just as profoundly, artists have documented the experience of everyday life, and the day-to-day struggles of ordinary people around the world.

Kazimir Malevich
Dynamic Suprematism 1915 or 1916

Malevich's abstract paintings belong to the intense period of artistic experimentation around the time of the 1917 Russian Revolution. In 1915 he abandoned representative images in favour of what he called suprematism. Initially he presented simple geometric forms – most famously a black square – against a white background that carried a suggestion of infinite space. *Dynamic Suprematism* is a more complex composition, with clusters of shapes and markings that seem to drift together or apart.

hands

teeth

eyes

Pablo Picasso
Weeping Woman 1937

In 1937, as a response to the Spanish Civil War, Picasso produced over forty images of a woman engulfed in tears. The figure originated in his mural *Guernica*, which depicted the devastating aerial bombardment of the small Basque town. *Weeping Woman* is the culmination of the series. The features of the woman were modelled on Picasso's then-partner Dora Maar, making this an intensely personal image, as well as an emblem of the suffering of the Spanish nation.

Malangatana Ngwenya
Untitled 1967

During the 1960s Malangatana took part in the struggle for independence in Mozambique. He was arrested by the Portuguese secret police and imprisoned for eighteen months. This work depicts the chaos and suffering of a society at war with itself. The figures overlap, seeming to merge into one another, filling the frame so that we have no sense of context or perspective. Instead the image is dominated by white gnashing teeth, claw-like hands and the wide eyes of humans and animals.

Saloua Raouda Choucair
Composition with Two Ovals 1951

Choucair was one of the few Lebanese artists of her generation to explore abstraction. Here the two ovals of the title are broken into smaller, boldly coloured forms, creating a dynamic rhythm of yellows, greens, greys and reds. The composition is given greater intensity by an unusually shaped canvas that seems both expansive in its width and confining in its height. Its sense of energy and movement pushes out against the edges of the frame.

Lygia Clark
Creature-Maquette (320) 1964

Brazilian artist Clark made a series of geometric, hinged-aluminium sculptures which she titled *Creatures* ('Bichos' in Portuguese), for which this is a working model. She compared the hinges to the intersecting bones of an animal skeleton. The sculptures were originally intended to be manipulated by hand, and could take many possible forms. Clark believed that the viewer's active participation was essential for the work.

Yinka Shonibare CBE
The British Library 2014

The British Library is a celebration of the vast, ongoing contribution made by migrants to British culture. The installation includes more than 6,000 books, specially bound in Dutch wax print fabric, a mass-produced imitation of Indonesian batik that is sold widely in Africa. Printed on the spines in gold letters are the names of first- or second-generation immigrants to Britain, from the sixth-century monk Augustine of Canterbury to the twenty-first-century footballer Danny Welbeck. Some books carry the names of people who have opposed immigration, while others remain unmarked, suggesting that the story of immigration in Britain is still being written.

Joseph Beuys
The End of the Twentieth Century 1983–5

This sculpture developed out of Beuys's project to plant 7,000 oak trees in Kassel, Germany, to encourage an 'ecological awakening' for humankind. A basalt stone was to be placed alongside each tree. Here, blocks of basalt lie scattered on the floor. Into each of the slabs, Beuys bored a conical hole to create a 'wound'. He then 'treated' it by smoothing and lining the hollow with insulating clay and felt, before re-inserting the stone. These filled cavities imply the potential for healing, suggesting the possibility of renewal at the end of a violent and destructive century.

Ellen Gallagher
Bird in Hand 2006

Sheets of inked and stained pages have been densely layered, then cut with a knife to reveal streaks of colour beneath. The result suggests an undersea landscape. At its centre is a one-legged pirate whose expansive growth of hair merges with the tendrils of vegetation that float around him, even as the thick undergrowth at his feet twines into and around his legs. The elaborate detail seems to multiply and grow through layers of paint, gold leaf, plasticine and rough rock crystal as well as paper elements that include maps, newspaper cuttings and advertisements for beauty products.

Lorna Simpson
Then & Now 2016

Simpson is known for her engagement with race and identity politics. This work was created by screen-printing two found photographs, after which the artist worked on the surface by hand. The photographs were taken during protests in Detroit in July 1967, which began after police attempted to arrest all eighty-two customers in an unlicensed bar. Over the next five days, forty-three people were killed, 1,189 injured and over 2,000 properties destroyed. Made at a time when police violence against African American citizens continues to dominate the headlines, Simpson's painting connects the events of 1967 to the present day.

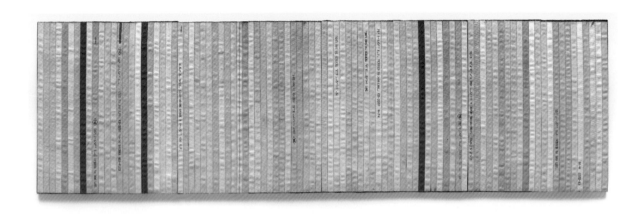

Theaster Gates
Civil Tapestry 4 2011

In May 1963, a group of African American school children and students were marching peacefully for equal rights in Birmingham, Alabama, when police used powerful fire hoses to break up the march, injuring many of the young protesters. Gates has arranged strips of decommissioned fire hoses to resemble the composition of a 1960s American abstract painting – a form that pointedly failed to engage with the Civil Rights movement. Gates also questions whether the protesters' goals have been fulfilled. 'Some of us are slightly better while others are a great deal better', he has reflected, 'but … things are far from equal.'

Teresa Margolles
Flag I 2009

The fabric of *Flag I* contains traces of blood, soil and other substances from the sites of murders around the northern border of Mexico. The work is a protest and an act of mourning for the thousands of violent deaths associated with the powerful drug cartels that control smuggling routes to the United States. For the artist, these were victims of the government's failure to intervene in the drug wars.

Richard Hamilton
The citizen 1981–3

When the British government revoked the Special Category status of IRA prisoners in 1976, inmates at the Maze prison in Northern Ireland began a series of protests. They first decided to wear only prison blankets, and then to carry out 'dirty protests' daubing their cell walls with excrement. *The citizen* was based on images from a 1980 news report and Hamilton wrote that, while he could not 'condone the methods' of the IRA, he was struck by the resemblance to images of Christian martyrdom.

MEDIA NETWORKS

This display explores some of the different ways in which artists have responded to the impact of mass media and communications, reflecting on a world increasingly shaped by advertising, television and digital technology.

The rapid pace of industrialisation, the unprecedented growth of cities, the speed of modern transportation, the cult of the machine, and revolutionary developments in communications technology all had an impact on the art of the early twentieth century. New approaches to painting and sculpture attempted to capture that sense of energy and excitement.

In the 1950s and 1960s the colourful imagery associated with comic books, advertising and Hollywood cinema had a similar impact, providing inspiration for pop art. Yet artists around the world approached such images in different ways. While many British and American artists seemed to wryly celebrate consumerism and the cult of celebrity, artists in Eastern Europe and Latin America were more directly subversive, and feminist artists challenged the gender stereotypes prevalent in the mass media.

Today, artists continue to engage with the new visual culture that is emerging from digital technology. Their responses can range from creating works that exist on internet platforms to exploring the instantaneous imagery of social media.

Umberto Boccioni
Unique Forms of Continuity in Space
1913, cast 1972

Boccioni was closely associated with futurism, an early twentieth-century movement that provocatively called for artists to reject old-fashioned ideas of beauty and celebrate the achievements of the machine age. The futurists were especially concerned with depicting motion. This is one of a series of striding sculptures, in which Boccioni represented movement as a continuous flowing form, like a blurred photograph.

Sonia Delaunay
Triptych 1963

Delaunay was a pioneer of abstract
painting, whose work extended beyond
fine art into fashion, textiles, costume
and set design, interior decoration,
architecture and advertising. She and
her artist husband Robert Delaunay
developed a distinctive approach to
abstraction called simultanism, exploring
how our perception of colours changes
when they are placed alongside each
other. This work was made when she was
in her late seventies. She called it *Triptych*
because it brings together three different
motifs that she had been working on.

Roy Lichtenstein
Whaam! 1963

In the 1960s, Lichtenstein made a series of paintings based on sources such as comic books, advertisements and mail-order catalogues. Recasting these small, mass-produced images as large-scale canvases, he would adjust the composition for greater dramatic effect, while still carefully imitating the appearance of the original printed materials. He was particularly drawn to war and romance comics, presenting their highly emotional subject matter in a detached, impersonal manner.

Evelyne Axell
Valentine 1966

The Belgian artist Axell was one of the first female European pop artists. *Valentine* is both a celebration of female sexuality and a tribute to the first woman in space, the Russian cosmonaut Valentina Tereshkova. The silhouette of a female figure is set against a gold background. Her pose is reminiscent of a 1960s pin-up, and the figure's sexuality is further emphasised by the real zip that runs down its front. On the opposite side of the canvas is a toy space helmet.

Guerrilla Girls
Do Women Have To Be Naked To Get Into the Met. Museum? 1989

The Guerrilla Girls are an anonymous activist group who highlight discrimination in the art world. Initially focusing on sexism, they have also addressed racism and other areas of social and gender-based inequality. Parodying a painting by the nineteenth-century French artist Jean-Auguste-Dominique Ingres, this poster first appeared as an advertisement on New York City buses, paid for by the Guerrilla Girls themselves, until the bus company cancelled it on grounds of indecency.

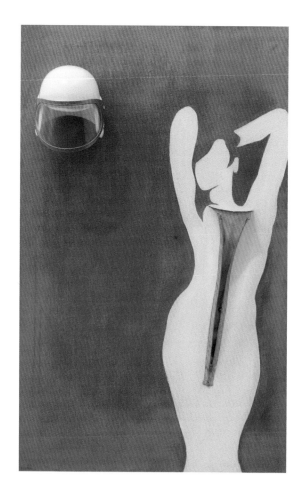

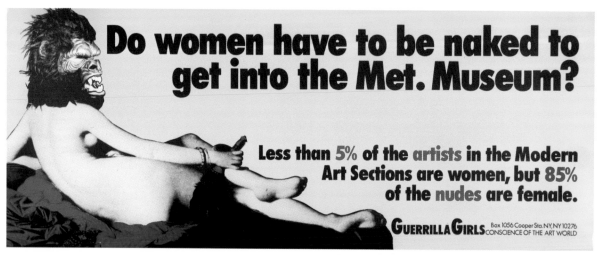

Barbara Kruger
Who owns what? 2012

Kruger's images grab the viewer's attention with an approach that is instantly recognisable, using found photographs that are cropped, manipulated and printed in black and white, and overlaid with text enclosed in a block of red. Directly addressing the viewer, her words challenge us to think about gender politics and the culture of consumerism.

The three simple words in *Who owns what?* can be placed into many different contexts, confronting the viewer with the numerous social faultlines created by inequality.

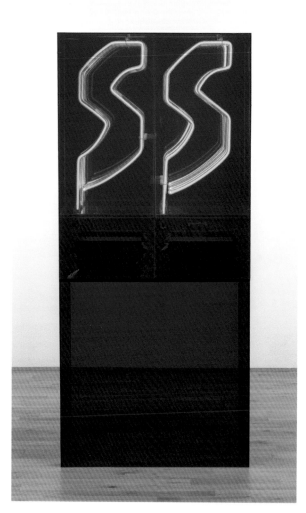

Chryssa
Study for Gates No. 4 1967

Born in Greece, Chryssa moved to New York in the 1950s. She loved the neon advertising in Times Square, and was one of the first artists to use neon lighting in her art. This work includes sixteen blue neon figures resembling the letter S and arranged in pairs. The lights flash on and off in a sequence. Their grey Plexiglas casing provides a dark background which, like the night sky, makes the neon shine more brightly.

Cildo Meireles
Babel 2001

Meireles refers to *Babel* as a 'tower of incomprehension'. Stacked with hundreds of radios, each tuned to a different station and adjusted to the minimum volume at which it is audible, the sculpture relates to the biblical story of the Tower of Babel, a tower tall enough to reach the heavens. God was affronted by this structure, and caused the builders to speak in different languages, so they became divided and scattered across the earth.

Peter Doig
Ski Jacket 1994

Ski Jacket was based on a newspaper photograph of skiers on a Japanese mountain. Doig has said he wanted to convey 'the way you perceive things when you are in the mountains ... how the light is often extreme and accentuated by wearing different coloured goggles'. The disorienting quality is emphasised as the painting was made on two panels of different widths. The two sides of the composition seem almost symmetrical – as if they were not quite mirror images of each other.

MATERIALS AND OBJECTS

Traditionally, certain materials have been associated with fine art in western Europe, whether applying oil paint to canvas, printing ink onto paper, or making sculpture from bronze, stone or wood. Over the last hundred years or so, however, artists have embraced a proliferation of alternative possibilities.

In the early years of the twentieth century, artists such as Pablo Picasso and Georges Braque began to use collage, combining paint with disparate materials such as newspapers, wallpaper patterns and advertisements. The principle of introducing elements from the real world was taken a step further by Marcel Duchamp's idea of the 'readymade' – an ordinary manufactured object that has been selected by the artist and designated as a work of art.

A different approach can be seen in the work of the Japanese mono-ha group. Rather than shaping or carving materials to impose their own vision on them, they wanted to open the viewer's eyes to the inherent qualities of the materials, and encouraged people to reflect on their relationship to their surroundings and to the natural world.

For today's artists, organic materials can be intertwined with mass-produced industrial products. There is a similar freedom in the techniques that are employed, whether using traditional craft techniques or impersonal manufacturing methods.

Marcel Duchamp
Fountain 1917, replica 1964

Fountain is the most famous of Duchamp's so-called 'readymades'. It was purchased from a sanitary ware supplier and submitted under the pseudonym R. Mutt to the newly established Society of Independent Artists in New York, which had pledged to promote and exhibit all varieties of modern art. As Duchamp may have anticipated, the Society rejected it, prompting a heated argument about whether it was a work of art or not.

Marisa Merz
Untitled (Living Sculpture) 1966

This large sculpture consists of twisted tubes of aluminium, stapled together and hung from the ceiling in fluid, swirling patterns. Merz was particularly concerned with the relationship between the sculpture and the space around it. The original version was made and installed by Merz in her home in Turin. As the title *Living Sculpture* implies, the construction developed by stages, generating an organic process of growth, like a plant that gradually engulfs its surroundings. The title may also refer to the sculpture's initial location in the artist's own living space. 'There has never been any division between my life and my work', Merz has said, and much of her work emerged from her idea of home as a private, intimate and feminine realm.

Lee Ufan
Relatum 1968, 1994

Ufan's sculptural works focus on the essential character and presence of their materials and their interconnections. Here he uses a single material – one hundred strips of stainless steel – and explores how the different elements relate to one another and to the space in which they are arranged. 'A work of art, rather than being a self-complete, independent entity, is a resonant relationship with the outside', he has said. 'It exists together with the world, simultaneously what it is and what it is not.'

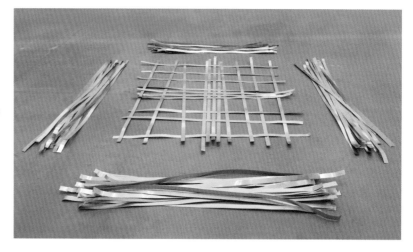

Susumu Koshimizu
From Surface to Surface
1971, remade 1976

From Surface to Surface investigates the substance of wood by sawing planks into different shapes, exposing their surface qualities through different kinds of repetitive cuts. In the late 1960s and early 1970s Koshimizu was associated with a group of Tokyo artists known as mono-ha, usually translated as the 'school of things'. Their work emphasised an attention to materials and explored the relationship between a sculpture and the surrounding space to make the viewer more aware of 'the world as it is'.

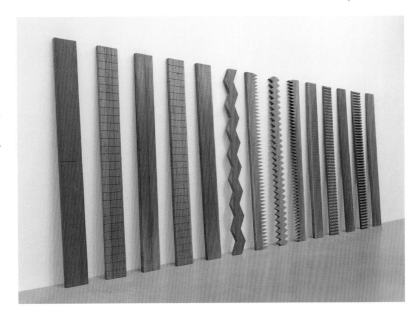

Mrinalini Mukherjee
Jauba 2000

Mukherjee was known for making sculptures using hemp rope – an everyday material in India. Weaving and knotting, she created complex shapes and folds that often resemble flowers or the body. *Jauba* is a Bengali word for the hibiscus flower. The hemp is dyed in bright colours and arranged around a freestanding metal support. Mukherjee was one of a number of women artists who established the importance of textiles and fibres as materials for making fine art.

Jannis Kounellis
Untitled 1968

Originally from Greece, Kounellis was associated with the Italian movement arte povera, which literally translates as 'poor art'. The arte povera artists approached art with absolute creative freedom. Bringing art closer to everyday life, they often used 'real' materials, ranging from plants and animals to common household items. Here four wooden bars have been loosely hung with wool, some of it dyed in shades of blue. Kounellis later suggested that he had pulled the wool out to resemble thick layers of paint dripping down a canvas.

Yuko Nasaka
Untitled 1964

Nasaka was one of the few female artists associated with the Gutai group. Based in Japan, the group placed a great emphasis on the process of making an artwork, sometimes turning that process into a public performance. For this work, Nasaka placed each plaster panel onto a mechanical turntable inspired by a potter's wheel. As it rotated, she carved patterns into the material using a palette knife. The recurring image of the circle suggests a timeless sense of harmony, while the dark-blue silver lacquer that she applied afterwards conveys a more industrial quality.

Mimmo Rotella
With a Smile 1962

In the early 1950s, Rotella began to rip posters away from the walls of outdoor hoardings in Rome, revealing the traces of other posters beneath. Many of the posters he chose were for films, but he also included advertisements for appliances and other goods, so that his works became a commentary on the post-war consumer boom. In the studio he would mount the poster fragments onto canvas, rearranging the pieces into new compositions but also stripping away further layers to accentuate their distressed appearance.

Haegue Yang
Sol LeWitt Upside Down – Structure with Three Towers, Expanded 23 Times, Split in Three 2015

Yang's installations are often created using everyday objects or items of furniture. This sculpture was built using more than 500 Venetian blinds; removed from their original function, they create an immersive environment. It relates to a floor-based sculpture by the American artist Sol LeWitt, made of open cubes arranged into three towers. Yang's version is significantly larger and is turned upside-down so that it hangs from the ceiling.

Sarah Sze
Seamless 1999 (detail)

Sze's ramshackle construction spreads throughout the room, burrowing into walls, twisting around corners, leaping across the doorway. A single interconnected entity, it was created using everyday items such as magnifying glasses, folding rulers, scissors, thimbles and measuring cups, attached with clamps, clothes-pegs and wire. The cheap, often plastic components link the work to contemporary consumer culture. However, there are also echoes of the abstract sculpture and painting of the early twentieth century, with the use of red, blue and yellow as a direct reference to the colours favoured by Piet Mondrian.

BLAVATNIK BUILDING

This new extension to Tate Modern was completed in 2016. Rising to ten floors, the variety of new spaces includes Tate Exchange, a dedicated centre for learning and engagement, and a viewing platform offering remarkable views across London. A new entrance to the south means that the museum now represents a link between the north and south of the city.

The new displays, entitled *How Art Became Active (1960 to Now)*, focus on developments over the last fifty or so years. Rather than regarding the artwork as a self-contained object, artists are thinking more dynamically about its relationship to the viewer, to the physical space around it, and its relationship to society.

At the base of the building are the Tanks, a space designed with live art, performance and expanded cinema in mind. Above that, level 2 is devoted to temporary exhibitions, level 3 explores performance and works that bring art closer to everyday life, while level 4 includes *Living Cities* and galleries dedicated to the *ARTIST ROOMS* programme – with a display that changes every year, looking in depth at a single artist.

not all levels open

PERFORMER
AND
PARTICIPANT

This display features artists who – in different ways –
have wanted to break down the boundaries between art
and real life.

Several of the works are based on performances, which
can involve generating a direct moment of communication
or confrontation between the artist and the audience.
These are represented on film, in photographs or
through sculptural props that imply certain actions
and movements.

There are also works that emerge from an artist's
engagement with a particular community or social group,
such as conducting research into social conditions or
recording people's memories. In other works, collective
actions emerge from traditional crafts or practices.

The display also includes installations that invite the
viewer's active participation, with environments to walk
through, spaces to explore and interactive elements, so
that the work becomes something to be experienced
rather than merely looked at.

Ana Lupas
The Solemn Process
1964–74/76; 1980–5; 1985–2008

In the 1960s, Romanian artist Lupas
worked with villagers in Transylvania to
create large structures inspired by the
local tradition of weaving wreaths for
harvest festivals. Made using natural
materials such as straw, hemp, cotton,
clay and wood, the individual objects
would decay, but the process of making
them continued from year to year. Over
time, however, as traditional skills
declined, Lupas found that fewer
participants were able to take part in her
project. Concerned to preserve the
structures, she sealed them into metal
casings – a solution that balanced the
natural and traditional with modern,
industrial techniques.

Edward Krasiński
Untitled 2001

Polish artist Krasiński's installation *Untitled* 2001 is a room that includes twelve suspended mirrors. A single line of blue tape runs all the way around the walls and across the surface of each mirror. This line, fixed at a height of 130 centimetres, links the different elements in the room but also creates a sense of continuity between the real space of the walls and the reflected space of the mirrors. Walking through this environment therefore conveys an extraordinary sense that your surroundings seem to expand and shrink around you, with your own reflected image becoming part of the scene.

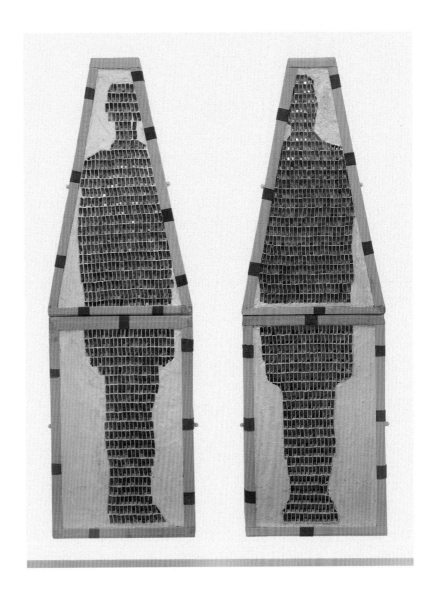

Paul Neagu
Great Tactile Table 1970

Neagu believed that the act of seeing had been corrupted by photography, cinema and television, and that artists should explore other senses, notably touch. Many of his works were intended to be handled. *Great Tactile Table* consists of hundreds of small boxes into which people could dip their fingers and experience different textures and substances. Arranged in the form of two figures, it is also a metaphor for the human body, which is also composed of different cells.

LIVING CITIES

The George Economou Gallery

This display looks at a variety of responses to the modern city, with artists from around the world exploring the urban landscape.

The perspectives range from panoramic overviews that attempt to map the whole city to close-up photographs recording the minutiae of daily life.

Above all, the city is seen as a fluid space that is always changing. Works deal with patterns of migration, and the different communities that emerge and adapt. The use of surprising materials such as rubber or couscous, or a focus on colours, encourages us to look at the city in imaginative new ways.

Julie Mehretu
Mogamma, A Painting in Four Parts: Part 3 2012

Mehretu's painting takes its name from a government building in Tahrir Square in Cairo. As a symbol of the Egyptian government it provided a focus for the 2011 protests against Hosni Mubarak's authoritarian regime. The painting is covered with overlapping architectural drawings of the Mogamma and other locations related to popular protest, such as Meskel Square in Addis Ababa and Zuccotti Park in New York, the site of the 'Occupy Wall Street' camp. On top of this, Mehretu has added a dense surface of marks and brushstrokes.

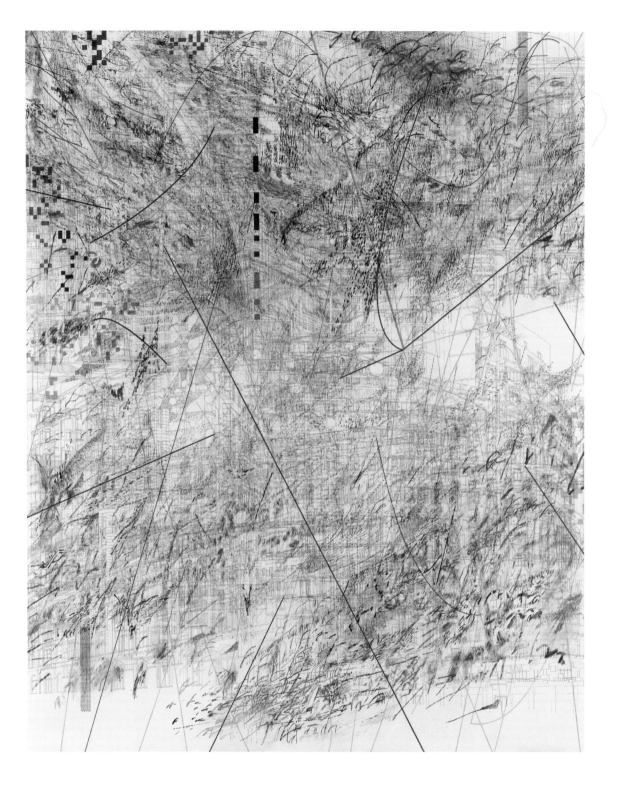

Monika Sosnowska
Pavilion 2016

Many of Sosnowska's sculptures explore
architecture and the ways in which
buildings are designed to embody social
and political values. *Pavilion* was inspired
by an innovative 1960s housing estate in
Lublin, Poland. The estate was designed
by the architects Zofia and Oskar Hansen,
whose theory of Open Form was intended
to encourage the creative participation of
the people who lived there. By the time
Sosnowska visited the estate it had fallen
into disrepair, its utopian ideals long
forgotten. In her sculpture the original
architecture has become twisted and
distorted, collapsed into sprawling chaos.

Mark Bradford
Los Moscos 2004

This vast collage consists of papers
gathered by the artist on the streets around
his studio in Los Angeles. The papers are
soaked, bleached, sanded and torn, then
pasted on top of each other. Stabs of
colour and fragmented words emerge
from the mass. The overall effect resembles
an aerial view of a city at night, with
pieces of yellow copier paper shining out
like areas of light. The title means 'the
flies' in Spanish. It derives from
derogatory local slang for the migrant
workers who gather every day, waiting for
construction jobs.

ARTIST ROOMS

Level 4 of the Blavatnik Building also presents works from *ARTIST ROOMS*, a collection that is jointly owned and managed by National Galleries of Scotland and Tate.

The collection gathers major groups of artworks by leading contemporary artists, so that whole rooms or exhibitions of their work can be made available to museums and galleries throughout the UK. The collection now includes more than 1,600 works. The *ARTIST ROOMS* galleries at Tate Modern began a series of year-long exhibitions with Louise Bourgeois in 2016, Bruce Nauman in 2017, Jenny Holzer in 2018 and Ed Ruscha in 2019.

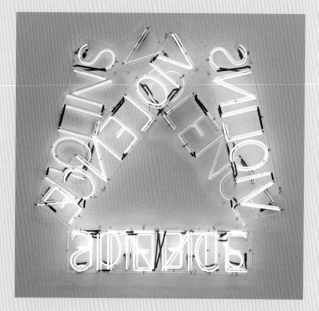

Opposite, top: Bruce Nauman
Violins Violence Silence 1981–2
(displayed 2017–18)

Opposite: Louise Bourgeois
Spider 1994 (displayed 2016–17)

Above: Jenny Holzer
Blue Purple Tilt 2007
(displayed 2018–19)

THE TANKS

Converted from the former oil tanks of Bankside Power
Station, these cavernous spaces form the foundation of
the Blavatnik Building.

Retaining their raw, industrial character, the Tanks are
designed to showcase live art, installation and the moving
image. In recent decades, artists have increasingly
engaged with areas such as performance, expanded
cinema, broadcast media, social activism, or works that
explore the relationship between artist and audience.
The Tanks provide an opportunity to look at the history
of these developments as well as current practice.

Wolfgang Tillmans, *South Tank Light Test* 2017

TATE BRITAIN
TATE LIVERPOOL
TATE ST IVES

Tate Britain is the home of British art from 1500 to the present day, including the world's largest collection of work by J.M.W. Turner. The free displays present a walk through the history of British art, with Spotlight rooms focusing on particular themes. As well as a stimulating exhibition programme, the gallery presents a major artistic commission in the Duveen galleries each year, and regularly hosts the Turner Prize.

Tate Liverpool is dedicated to international modern and contemporary art. Opening in 1988, the building was converted from a former warehouse on the Albert Dock, once a key hub for international trade. With an active education programme, the gallery encourages a new, younger audience. Major exhibitions have included surveys of work by Jackson Pollock, Andy Warhol, Francis Bacon, Sarah Lucas, Gustav Klimt and Piet Mondrian.

Tate St Ives is located on the coast of Cornwall, in a town whose unique landscape and quality of light have attracted artists since Victorian times. Overlooking Porthmeor Beach and facing out to the Atlantic Ocean, the gallery celebrates the remarkable variety of artists who lived or worked in the area, including Alfred Wallis, Ben Nicholson, Naum Gabo and Barbara Hepworth, whose former studio is now a Museum and Sculpture Garden managed by Tate.

CREDITS

Abboud: Purchased with funds provided by the Middle East North Africa Acquisitions Committee 2014. © Succession Shafic Abboud

Axell: Purchased with funds provided by Tate International Council 2016. © ADAGP, Paris / DACS, London 2019

Barlow: ARTIST ROOMS Tate and National Galleries of Scotland. Presented by the artist and acquired with assistance from the ARTIST ROOMS Endowment, supported by the Henry Moore Foundation and Tate Members 2015. © Courtesy the artist

Beuys: Purchased with assistance from Edwin C. Cohen and Echoing Green 1991. © DACS, 2019

Boccioni: Purchased 1972

Bourgeois: ARTIST ROOMS. Tate and National Galleries of Scotland. Lent by the Easton Foundation 2013. © The Easton Foundation/ VAGA (p.58); Lent by the Tate Americas Foundation, courtesy The Easton Foundation in honour of Frances Morris 2016. On long term loan. © The Easton Foundation / VAGA at ARS, NY and DACS (p.16)

Braque: Purchased 1966. © ADAGP, Paris and DACS, London 2019

Bruguera: Purchased with funds provided by Alin Ryan von Buch 2009. © Tania Bruguera

Choucair: Purchased with funds provided by the Middle East North Africa Acquisitions Committee 2011. © Saloua Raouda Choucair Foundation

Chryssa: Presented by S. Herbert Meller through the American Federation of Arts 1968. © Chryssa Vardea

Clark: Presented by the American Fund for the Tate Gallery 2012. © Courtesy of 'The World of Lygia Clark' Cultural Association

Dalí: Purchased 1979. © Salvador Dalí, Fundació Gala-Salvador Dalí, DACS 2019

Dean: Purchased with assistance from Tate Members 2014. © Tacita Dean, courtesy Frith Street Gallery, London and Marian Goodman Gallery, New York/Paris

Delaunay: Purchased 1966. © Pracusa 2016

Doig: Purchased with assistance from Evelyn, Lady Downshire's Trust Fund 1995. © Peter Doig. All rights reserved, DACS, 2019

Duchamp: Purchased with assistance from the Friends of the Tate Gallery 1999. © Association Marcel Duchamp/ADAGP, Paris and DACS, London 2019

Eliasson: The Unilever Series, Turbine Hall, Tate Modern 2003. © Olafur Eliasson

El-Salahi: Purchased from the artist with assistance from the Africa Acquisitions Committee, the Middle East North Africa Acquisitions Committee, Tate International Council and Tate Members 2013. © Ibrahim El-Salahi

Fini: Presented by Tate Members 2011. © ADAGP, Paris and DACS, London 2019

Floyer: Purchased 2009. © Ceal Floyer, courtesy Lisson Gallery, London

Gallagher: Presented anonymously 2007. © Ellen Gallagher

Gates: Presented by Pamela J. Joyner and Alfred J. Giuffrida (Tate Americas Foundation) 2014. © Theaster Gates

Gonzalez-Foerster: The Unilever Series, Turbine Hall, Tate Members, 2008. © ADAGP, Paris and DACS, London 2019

Guerrilla Girls: Purchased 2003. © Courtesy www.guerrillagirls.com

Hamilton: Purchased 1985. © The estate of Richard Hamilton

Hesse: Purchased 1979. © The estate of Eva Hesse, courtesy Hauser & Wirth, Zürich

Höller: The Unilever Series, Turbine Hall, Tate Members, 2006. © DACS 2019

Holzer: ARTIST ROOMS Acquired jointly with the National Galleries of Scotland through The d'Offay Donation with assistance from the National Heritage Memorial Fund and the Art Fund 2008. © Jenny Holzer, member/Artists Rights Society (ARS), New York.

Kapoor: The Unilever Series, Turbine Hall, Tate Members, 2002. © Anish Kapoor. All Rights Reserved, DACS 2019

Koshimizu: Purchased with funds provided by the Asia Pacific Acquisitions Committee 2008. © Susumu Koshimizu

Kounellis: Purchased 1996. © Jannis Kounellis

Krasner: Purchased 1981. © The Pollock-Krasner Foundation ARS, NY and DACS

Krasiński: Presented by Tate Members 2007. © The estate of Edward Krasiński, courtesy Foksal Gallery Foundation, Warsaw

Kruger: Purchased with assistance from the Karpidas Family (Tate Americas Foundation) 2013. © Barbara Kruger

Lichtenstein: Purchased 1966. © Estate of Roy Lichtenstein/ DACS 2019

Lupas: Purchased with funds provided by the Russia and Eastern Europe Acquisitions Committee 2016. © Ana Lupas

Malevich: Purchased with assistance from the Friends of the Tate Gallery 1978.

Matisse: Purchased with assistance from the Friends of the Tate Gallery 1962. © Succession H. Matisse /DACS 2019

Margolles: Presented by the Tate Americas Foundation, courtesy of the Latin American Acquisitions Committee 2015. © The Artist and Galene Peter Kilchmann, Zurich

Mehretu: Purchased with funds provided by Tiqui Atencio Demirdjian and Ago Demirdjian, Andreas Kurtz and the Tate Americas Foundation 2014. © Julie Mehretu. Courtesy the artist and the Marian Goodman Gallery

Meireles: Purchased jointly by Tate, London (with the assistance of the Latin American Acquisitions Committee) and the D.Daskalopoulos Collection, 2013, as a promised gift to Tate. © Cildo Meireles. Courtesy Galerie Lelong, New York

Merz: Purchased with funds provided by an anonymous donor 2009. © Marisa Merz

Mukherjee: Purchased with funds provided by the South Asia Acquisitions Committee 2015. © Estate of the artist

Nasaka: Purchased with funds provided by the Asia Pacific Acquisitions Committee 2017. © The Artist and Axel Vervoordt Gallery

Nauman: ARTIST ROOMS Tate and National Galleries of Scotland. Lent by Anthony d'Offay 2010. On long term loan. © Bruce Nauman/ Artists Rights Society (ARS), New York and DACS, London 2019

Neagu: Purchased 2000. © Estate of Paul Neagu

Ngwenya: Purchased with funds provided by the Africa Acquisitions Committee 2014. © Estate of Malangatana Ngwenya

Picasso: Accepted by HM Government in lieu of tax with additional payment (Grant-in-Aid) made with assistance from the National Heritage Memorial Fund, the Art Fund and the Friends of the Tate Gallery 1987. © Succession Picasso/DACS, London 2019

Procter: Presented by the Daily Mail 1927. © Tate

Salcedo: Presented by the artist, White Cube, London and Alexander and Bonin, New York 2008. © Doris Salcedo

Richier: Presented by the artist's estate 2000. © The estate of Germaine Richier

Richter: Presented by Tate Members 2015. © ADAGP, Paris and DACS, London 2019

Reigl: Presented by Winifred Miller and Cecilia Kerr 2006. © Judit Reigl

Rothko: Presented by the artist through the American Federation of Arts 1969. © 1998 Kate Rothko Prizel & Christopher Rothko ARS, NY and DACS, London

Shonibare: Purchased with Art Fund support and funds provided by the Tate International Council, the Africa Acquisitions Committee, Wendy Fisher and THE EKARD COLLECTION 2019. © Yinka Shonibare. Co-commissioned by HOUSE 2014 and Brighton Festival. Courtesy the artist and Stephen Friedman Gallery, London.

Simpson: Lent by the Tate Americas Foundation, purchased using endowment income 2017. On long term loan. © Lorna Simpson, courtesy Salon 94, New York

Sosnowska: Purchased with funds provided by the Russia and Eastern Europe Acquisitions Committee 2017. © Monika Sosnowska

Sze: Presented by Edwin Cohen and Dillon Cohen (Tate Americas Foundation) 2018. On long term loan. © Sarah Sze

Tillmans: South Tank, 2017. © Wolfgang Tillmans, Courtesy Maureen Paley, London

Ufan: Purchased with funds provided by the Asia Pacific Acquisitions Committee 2015. © Lee Ufan

Whiteread: The Unilever Series, Turbine Hall, Tate Modern, 2005. © Rachel Whiteread

Weiwei: The Unilever Series, Turbine Hall, Tate Modern, 2008. © Ai Weiwei

Yang: Purchased with funds provided by the Asia Pacific Acquisitions Committee and Kyung-soo Huh, Sung-Moon Kwon, Tae Won Hahn and Byucksan Foundation 2018. © Haegue Yang

Photographic credits:

Photography is © Tate Photography 2019 unless otherwise stated.

Courtesy Foksal Gallery Foundation; Galerie Peter Kilchmann 52; Photo © Ian Kingsnorth 62 right; Courtesy Ana Lupas, photo: Rainer Iglar / installation at Galerie im Taxispalais / Galerie des Landes Tirol, Innsbruck 51; © Gerhard Richter 2019 (29052019) 11; Photo: John Riddye 5 top left; Courtesy Sprüth Magers 37; © Tate, 2019 / Andrew Dunkley 3, 38, 42 bottom, 47, 48–9; / Mark Heathcote 14, 43 bottom; / Mark Heathcote and Rose Hillson Summers 27 bottom; / Joe Humphrys 35; / Marcus Leith 6–7, 42 top, 43 top, 59; / Marcus Leith and Andrew Dunkley 4, 5 centre left and right, 5 bottom centre, 5 bottom right, 30, 31 left; / Seraphina Neville 56, 60–1; © Tate Liverpool / Roger Sinek 62 left; Courtesy Ai Weiwei Studio, 5.

Tate is a charity and relies on a large number of supporters – individuals, foundations, companies and public sector sources – to enable it to deliver its programme of activities, both on and off its gallery sites. This support is essential in order for Tate to acquire works of art for the Collection, run education, outreach and exhibition programmes, care for the Collection in storage and enable art to be displayed, both digitally and physically, inside and outside Tate. For more information, please visit: www.tate.org.uk/join-support

First published 2016 by order of the Tate Trustees by Tate Publishing, a division of Tate Enterprises Ltd,Millbank, London SW1P 4RG www.tate.org.uk/publishing

This revised edition published 2019

© Tate Enterprises Ltd 2019

ISBN 978 1 84976 667 8

Written by Simon Bolitho, Curator, Interpretation, Tate Modern

Project Editor: Emilia Will

Colour reproduction by DL Imaging, London

Printed and bound by Cambrian Printers, Wales

Also available

Tate Britain Highlights (ISBN 978 1 84976 580 0)